G000147160

YORKSHIRE

Compiled by Adrian Braddy

Published in Great Britain in 2017 by Dalesman
an imprint of
Country Publications Ltd
The Water Mill, Broughton Hall, Skipton BD23 3AG

A British Cataloguing in Publication record is
available for this book

ISBN: 978-1-85568-364-8

Printed in Europe for Latitude Press Ltd.

INTRODUCTION

Yorkshire is many things to many people but it is certainly not little.

England's greatest county is home to landscapes, culture and people as diverse as any comparable location on the planet. Squeezing the essence of all that into a single volume is not easy.

For our first *Little Book of Yorkshire* we had a good stab at it, gathering together almost as many nuggets of Tykeish treasure as there are leaves in a Yorkshire teabag. Inevitably, however, there was so much we simply did not have space to include.

This second pocket-sized volume of Yorkshire delights includes many of the words of wisdom, phrases, sayings, jokes and trivia collected from around the White Rose County that we could not find space for in the first.

It is our hope that each turn of the page will elicit another smile of recognition in anyone who loves God's Own Country.

So, as you begin to browse the pint-sized pages that follow, prepare to glow with Yorkshire pride.

Adrian Braddy

Being from Yorkshire is as much a state of mind as a geographical fact.

LIAM ALLEN

I've always been very proud of the fact I was born in Yorkshire because it's one of the few counties that has a very definable sense of itself.

JEREMY PAXMAN

DID YOU KNOW?

If Yorkshire were a country, it would
have finished 12th in the medals
table at the 2012 Olympic Games.
It picked up seven gold medals,
two silver and three bronze. *The
Guardian* joked, "we can expect
a hosting bid from Wetwang in
2020". In 2016 Yorkshire would
have finished 17th, ahead of New
Zealand, Canada and South Africa.

Rome wasn't built in a day, but then
again I wasn't on that particular job.

BRIAN CLOUGH

DID YOU KNOW?

Yorkshire is not only home to the world's oldest sweet shop (in Pateley Bridge), it is also where the best-known sweets were created. KitKat, Chocolate Orange, Quality Street, Smarties, Aero, Jelly Babies, Fox's Biscuits, Thornton chocolates, Fruit Pastilles, After Eights, Yorkies, Lion bars, Toffee Crisps, Caramac, Liquorice Allsorts, Sherbert Lemons, Pear Drops and Dolly Mixture are some of the delights born in the White Rose county.

I'm from Yorkshire.
I'm the full Brontë.

BARRY CRYER

I don't speak French. I don't speak English. I am from Yorkshire.

GEOFFREY BOYCOTT

The flowers of Yorkshire are like the women of Yorkshire. Every stage of their growth has its own beauty, but the last phase is always the most glorious. Then, very quickly, they all go to seed.

CALENDAR GIRLS

The man who wants to lead
the orchestra must turn his back
on the crowd.

CAPTAIN JAMES COOK

The Yorkshireman has, no doubt, a way of speaking his mind very freely, and telling you what he thinks. However unpleasant this habit may be at times, it has its advantages; you at least know where you are with them and you can always tell whether a Yorkshireman likes or dislikes what you do – he as good as tells you.

YORKSHIRE FOLK-TALK, 1892

I can quite see why some Yorkshiremen give the place a bad name. But we're not all insensitive to other people's feelings, and we don't all grow up with enough arrogance to fuel an army. Some of us remain reassuringly baffled by life and far too sensitive for our own good.

ALAN TITCHMARSH

DID YOU KNOW?

Christmas wouldn't be Christmas without Yorkshire. It is said that the first Christmas festival ever held in Britain took place in AD 521 in York. Meanwhile, William Strickland, of Boynton, near Bridlington, is believed to have introduced the turkey to England in the mid-sixteenth century. And the first use of the term Hogmanay has been traced not to Scotland but to Methley, near Leeds.

It is a Yorkshire habit to say what
you think with blunt frankness.

FRANCES HODGSON BURNETT,
THE SECRET GARDEN

Did you know?

In Yorkshire we have many ways to describe the rain – after all, we have more than our fair share. Here are just a few examples:

chuckin it dahn, peshin it dahn, teemin doon, tipplin dahn, silin dahn.

When it starts to rain, it's "comin on".

DID YOU KNOW?

The world's first moving film was
shot in Leeds in 1888.

Did you know?

Yorkshire has long been the first choice for holidaymakers. It is home to both England's first seaside resort (Scarborough) and England's oldest tourist attraction (Mother Shipton's Cave).

I do feel British first, then I feel Scottish, then I feel Yorkshire and I feel English a long, long way behind that.

ALASTAIR CAMPBELL

I don't do impersonations. I can do a wounded elephant! I can do a really good cow! And because of the amount of time I spent in North Yorkshire, I do a variety of sheep. All of which I will be happy to roll out for you!

PATRICK STEWART

DID YOU KNOW?

Hull is home to what is said to be England's smallest window. It's part of the George Hotel, situated on the narrow street called the Land of Green Ginger.

Did you know?

The world's largest glass of beer was brewed in Halifax in July 2014. The glass measured 7ft 4in (2.23m) tall. It took an hour to fill the glass, which contained 3,664 pints (2,082 litres).

DID YOU KNOW?

Scenes from *The King's Speech* set at Wembley Stadium were actually filmed in Yorkshire – at Elland Road, Leeds, and Odsal Stadium, Bradford. Hundreds of inflatable people helped fill out the seats.

DID YOU KNOW?

The first British astronaut was a Yorkshirewoman. Dr Helen Sharman, born in Sheffield, became the first woman to visit the Mir space station in 1991.

My sister Emily loved the moors. Flowers brighter than the rose bloomed in the blackest of the heath for her; out of a sullen hollow in a livid hillside her mind could make an Eden. She found in the bleak solitude many and dear delights; and not the least and best-loved was – liberty.

Charlotte Brontë

An Honest Yorkshireman

Ah is i' truth a coontry youth,
Nean used to Lunnon fashions;
Yet vartue guides, an' still presides
Ower all my steps an' passions.
Nea coortly leer, bud all sincere,
Nea bribe shall iver blinnd me ;
If thoo can like a Yorkshire tike,
A rogue thoo'll niver finnd me.

HENRY CAREY

Yorkshire is much the biggest county in England, indeed clearly a "country", a diverse geographical entity of great cities, ancient cathedrals, industrial estates, seats of learning, wild uplands and sweeping coasts. Its natural landscape is as varied as any in Europe, from the raw limestone Pennines to the spreading Vale of York, from the lush dales to the bare Cleveland Hills.

SIMON JENKINS

I [your name], being resident in the [East/North/West] Riding of Yorkshire, declare: that Yorkshire is three Ridings and the City of York with these boundaries of 1142 years standing; that the address of all places in these Ridings is Yorkshire; that all persons born therein or resident therein and loyal to the Ridings are Yorkshire men and women; That any person or corporate body which deliberately ignores or denies the aforementioned shall forfeit all claim to Yorkshire status.

These declarations made this Yorkshire Day. God Save the Queen!

YORKSHIRE DECLARATION OF IDENTITY, DECLARED ON YORKSHIRE DAY (1ST AUGUST ANNUALLY)

One musician from Dalton, Kirklees
Had extr'ordinary knobbly knees.
They were hired for percussion
And caused much discussion
And earned him a packet in fees!

LISA SPEIGHT, WINNER, BEST LOCAL
LIMERICK AWARDS 2007

LAUGHTER LINES

Mamma Mia: classic ABBA song or a Yorkshire child telling his mother he's arrived?

LAUGHTER LINES

A Yorkshireman goes to a jeweller's and asks, "Can tha mek us a gold statue o' me whippet?"

The goldsmith says he can, then asks: "Do you want it eighteen carat?"

The man replies: "Nay lad, chewin' a bone'll do fine."

I love the drive from York to Whitby over the moors – one of the great journeys, in my book.

PENELOPE WILTON

How rich is our country in rivers;
in little dales and mighty dales;
in crumbling castles, in abbeys
and priories, in inns and sturdy
villages; in scrambling walls and
rugged roads; in boulders, screes
and scars; in noble halls and
pleasances; in lonely tarns, in moor
and mountain, in wild birds, in
tumbling ghylls, in gnarled oaks and
ash and thorns, in firs and pines;
in generous food; in lusty lads and

lasses; in short – for my breath fails me – in every decent thing the heart of man could desire.

ALFRED J BROWN

When God had finished making Heaven, rather like you make an apple pie, with that bit of pastry that was left over, he fashioned the Yorkshire Dales.

RUSSELL HARTY

I wish I were a girl again, half savage and hardy, and free... Why am I so changed? I'm sure I should be myself were I once among the heather on those hills.

EMILY BRONTË,
WUTHERING HEIGHTS

It is absolutely impossible for any of us, no matter how fond we may be of our native county, to comprehend its vast size.

J S Fletcher

I like Yorkshire Tea – very strong and English.

ELSA PERETTI

When Yorkshire's choral sons their
powers unite

Their tones astonish and their
chords delight

Healthful and strong, their voices
may defy

In strength all singers else beneath
the sky.

JOHN NICHOLSON

Did you know?

Last of the Summer Wine is the longest-running situation comedy in the world. The Holmfirth-filmed series ran for 295 episodes between 1973 and 2010. Every episode was written by Austerfield-born Roy Clarke.

No other county produces so much originality – and that originality, when carried to excess, is eccentricity.

SABINE BARING-GOULD

Here's tiv him be he tyke or
Foreigner whee can truly say
He was nivver maesthered
By owther hoss or woman.

YORKSHIRE TOAST

I love Yorkshire and Yorkshire people. I admire them for their bluntness … if you want to know your shortcomings, you won't find more helpful people anywhere.

BILL BRYSON

By comparison with places like Yorkshire or Northumberland, the counties of southern England scarcely exist. Who knows – who cares? – where Berkshire ends and Hampshire begins? Any self-respecting Yorkshireman knows precisely which towns are inside his county and which have the misfortune to lie in outer darkness.

JEREMY PAXMAN

I lingered round them, under that benign sky: watched the moths fluttering among the heath and harebells, listened to the soft wind breathing through the grass, and wondered how any one could ever imagine unquiet slumbers for the sleepers in that quiet earth.

EMILY BRONTË,
WUTHERING HEIGHTS

DID YOU KNOW?

Britain's earliest house was found in 2010 near Scarborough. Dating back 11,500 years to the Stone Age, it is so old that it was built when Britain was still attached to Continental Europe.

A Yorkshireman in the South will always take care to let you know that he regards you as an inferior. If you ask him why, he will explain that it is only in the North that life is 'real' life, that the industrial work done in the North is the only 'real' work, that the North is inhabited by 'real' people, the South merely by rentiers and their parasites. The Northerner has 'grit', he is grim, 'dour', plucky, warm-hearted, and democratic; the Southerner is

snobbish, effeminate, and lazy—
that at any rate is the theory.
Hence the Southerner goes north,
at any rate for the first time, with
the vague inferiority-complex of
a civilized man venturing among
savages, while the Yorkshireman,
like the Scotchman, comes to
London in the spirit of a barbarian
out for loot.

GEORGE ORWELL,
THE ROAD TO WIGAN PIER

The Doctor: I've run restaurants. Who do you think invented Yorkshire pudding?

Rory Williams: You didn't.

The Doctor: Pudding yet savoury. Sound familiar?

DOCTOR WHO: THE POWER OF THREE, 2012

DID YOU KNOW?

Both the cat's eye and the zebra crossing were invented by Yorkshiremen.

LAUGHTER LINES

Wrigley's has launched a new website where you can order chewing gum online. It's called ebuygum.com

The thing about Yorkshire people
is that they will tell you point blank
whether they like something or not.

KAY MELLOR

Glimpses were to be caught of
a roast leg of pork, bursting
into tears of sage and onion in a
metal reservoir full of gravy, of
an unctuous piece of roast beef
and blisterous Yorkshire pudding
bubbling hot in a similar receptacle.

LITTLE DORRIT, CHARLES DICKENS

Am I a sexist? No, I'm Yorkshire.

MICHAEL PARKINSON

I'd rather be a professional Yorkshireman than an amateur Lancashireman.

IAN MCMILLAN

Have you ever heard of an amateur Yorkshireman?

Paul Routledge

DID YOU KNOW?

Brian Robinson, of Huddersfield,
was the first Briton to finish the
Tour de France and the first to
win a Tour stage. Fellow cyclist
Beryl Burton, of Morley, was world
champion five times.

The way to the railway was all down hill over smooth, short turf with here and there furze bushes and grey and yellow rocks sticking out like candied peel from the top of a cake. The way ended in a steep run and a wooden fence – and there was the railway with the shining metals and the telegraph wires and posts and signals.

E NESBIT, *THE RAILWAY CHILDREN*

Even a Lancastrian has to admit that Yorkshire has given much to the world.

BRIAN GROOM, *FINANCIAL TIMES*

Did you know?

Morrisons, ASDA and Marks &
Spencer all started life in Yorkshire.

She is much bound to the singular
love and motherly care of Nature,
in placing her under so temperate
a clime, that in every measure
she is indifferently fruitful. If one
part of her be stone, and a sandy
barren ground, another is fertile
and richly adorned with corn-
fields. If you here find it naked and
destitute of woods, you shall see it
there shadowed with forests full of
trees, that have very thick bodies,
sending forth many fruitful and

profitable branches. If one place of it be moorish, miry, and unpleasant, another makes a free tender of delight, and presents itself to the eye full of beauty and contentive variety.

John Speed

Yorkshire has around 18,900 miles (30,430km) of drystone walls, more than a quarter of England's total; enough to encircle the British Isles coastline if laid end to end.

COUNTRYSIDE AGENCY

Let London still the just
precedence claim,

York ever shall be proud to be the
next in fame.

Scottish poet

Yorkshire is infinite, and contains multitudes, and is a house that has many, many rooms in and so it's easy to write about Yorkshire, really easy.

IAN MCMILLAN

DID YOU KNOW?

Sir George Cayley, of Scarborough, is known as the 'father of aviation'. He created the first man-carrying glider, and many consider him to be the first person to understand the underlying principles and forces of flight.

Yorkshire – it's even better than we thought!

HEADLINE IN *THE GUARDIAN*, 29 OCTOBER, 2013

Harrogate may soon be changing its name to 'Happygate', as it has been named the happiest place to live for the third year in a row.

RIGHTMOVE REPORT, 2015

Asked by Yorkshire Tea if I would like "a quick jaunt to King's Cross Station" to have my face modelled in cake and put on a plinth in the forecourt. It's not a distinction that is to be conferred on me alone, though Yorkshire Tea does not specify who my fellow *modèles en gâteaux* might be – the late Freddie Trueman I would guess, Michael Parkinson possibly and Alan Titchmarsh (who's so amiable he might even do it). A candidate for pâtisserie posterity would once have been that son of Yorkshire Jimmy Savile, who seemed made from marzipan. But not now. No cake for James.

ALAN BENNETT

O Swardill's good for horses,
An' Wensla-dill for cheese
And Airdill folk are busy as a bee;
But wheesoe're I wander,
My owd heart aye grows fonder
O' Whardill wheer I'll lig me doon
an' dee.

F W Moorman

We have had for breakfast toast, cakes, a Yorkshire pie, a piece of beef about the size and much the shape of my portmanteau, tea, coffee, ham and eggs.

CHARLES DICKENS DESCRIBES YORKSHIRE HOSPITALITY IN A LETTER TO HIS WIFE, 1838

DID YOU KNOW?

The oldest chemist's shop in England can be found in Knaresborough. Founded around 1720, it included a bleeding couch used during the application of leeches.

In 2017, Adam Heyton of Horsforth broke the world record for the number of countries visited in twenty-four hours using only planes, trains and buses.

With a population as big as Scotland's and an area half the size of Belgium, Yorkshire is almost a country in itself. It has its own flag, its own dialect and its own celebration, Yorkshire Day (1 August). While local folk are proud to be English, they're even prouder to be natives of 'God's Own County'. What makes Yorkshire so special? First, there's the landscape – with its brooding moors and green dales rolling down to a dramatic coastline, Yorkshire has some of Britain's finest scenery. Second, there's the sheer breadth of history – every facet of the British experience is represented here, from Roman times to the 21st century.

But Yorkshire's greatest appeal lies in its people. Industrious and opinionated, they have a wry wit and shrewd friendliness. Stay here for a while and you'll come away believing, like the locals, that God is indeed a Yorkshirewoman.

LONELY PLANET

I was struck by the beauty of Yorkshire and difference between it in summer and winter, as well as the contrast between what a great city Leeds is and the beautiful countryside which is only a few kilometres away. It's really fascinating.

CHRISTIAN PRUDHOMME,
DIRECTOR OF LE TOUR DE FRANCE

The Pennine Way … Great
North Roof.

IVOR BROWN

We shall be remiss if we do not recognise the Yorkshire gene. It explains what we are.

Of course, the gene is being weakened by the diaspora of families and intermarriage with lesser mortals. But in its pure form it is to be found in the wonderful, stubborn awkwardness of the true Yorkshireman.

What else could have created Captain Cook, William Wilberforce or John Harrison, who saved countless sailors' lives by finding a way to fix longitude in the face of scientific elitism? Or, for that matter, John Wycliffe, who battled against church abuse, or William Bateson, founder of genetics, and Sir Almroth Edward Wright, the pioneer of immunisation, both of whom took no prisoners in argument? And what about Guy Fawkes and Baroness Betty Boothroyd, whose downright refusal to take "No" for an answer from constituencies eventually saw a Tiller Girl as Speaker of the House of Commons Fawkes wanted to blow up with the rest of the Palace of Westminster?

I rest my case – and I haven't mentioned Harvey Smith or Geoffrey Boycott or the late Brian Clough.

SIR BERNARD INGHAM

Auction of Promises: Lot 7:
trip with the City of York's
road-gritting team.

YORK EVENING PRESS

There's one good thing abaht bein' poor – it costs nowt.

OLD AMOS

A Yorkshireman's heart is like his pudding – crisp outside, but soft within.

W R Mitchell

The countryside, particularly in Swaledale, is bathed in sunshine and looks spectacular, especially from a helicopter, though since part of the object of the exercise is to fetch more tourists in, I have mixed feelings about its attractions.

ALAN BENNETT ON THE TOUR DE FRANCE YORKSHIRE GRAND DÉPART

A short-sighted cyclist at York,
Was teaching his parrot to talk.
When perched on his neck
It gave him a peck;
The cyclist fell off with a squawk.

ANON

DID YOU KNOW?

Yorkshire has inspired much of the world's greatest children's literature – *The Railway Children*, *The Secret Garden*, *The Water Babies*… and the *Mr Men*. The latter were the creation of Cleckheaton-born Roger Hargreaves.

LAUGHTER LINES

An old man from Hawes paid his first visit to London and stood outside the Mansion House watching traffic. A policeman remarked: "Busy, isn't it?" "Aye," said the old man. "There's a trip in frae Hawes."

An amorous boatman of Staithes
Catches fishes whenever he bathes,
The fish fill his larder
The sea cools his ardour
Oh, pity the poor females of
Staithes.

ANON

We shall never really understand the Pennine dalespeople until we realise their pre-occupation with sheep.

ELLA PONTEFRACT

Dahn at heels, aht at toes,
Aht o' work, an i' owd close,
Short o' brass, friends few,
then it's winter.

**FROM AN OLD YORKSHIRE
NEWSPAPER**

LAUGHTER LINES

"How's business?"

"Terrible – even them 'at don't intend to pay aren't buying owt."

"Will you buy your wife a present?"

"Maybe I'll let her have a look in the Argos catalogue."

£22M LOTTERY WINNER TERRY BENSON, FROM HULL

I was always very proud of living in the West Riding of Yorkshire, in that hilly part which is called the backbone of England, the Pennine Chain… At night I loved to see the lighted trams climbing up the dark hills like fireflies on dark velvet; it seemed to me that they were brave and sturdy, like Yorkshire people, not afraid of difficult tasks or big hills.

Phyllis Bentley

A man in a railway compartment said he could tell where each passenger came from simply by hearing them speak. At length, he turned to a man sitting moping in the corner. "You're the easiest of the lot; you're from Lancashire." The man bestirred himself and said: "Nay, Ah'm from Yorkshire really. But Ah've bin nobbut badly for three week."

W R Mitchell

High waving heather, 'neath stormy
blasts bending,

Midnight and moonlight and bright
shining stars;

Darkness and glory rejoicingly
blending,

Earth rising to heaven and heaven
descending,

Man's spirit away from its drear
dongeon sending,

Bursting the fetters and breaking
the bars.

EMILY BRONTË

A Yorkshire banquet – bread and cheese and a chap you can talk to.

ANON

LAUGHTER LINES

Cockney: They're all a bit fick up nawth, ain't they?

Yorkshireman: Ah've allus bin told t'densest population were in London.

There's always that pride of saying 'I was born in Yorkshire'. You never try and hide it. There's a pride there, and Yorkshire people down south who've lost their accent, when they meet a fellow Yorkshireman it's almost like being in a lifelong club, the British Legion or something. It's like a badge.

TONY CHRISTIE

There's an old saying in Yorkshire, you know: it's nice to be important but it's more important to be nice.

PAUL SHANE

Wind? They should have a notice in these parts: "Beware of low-flying sheep".

HEARD AT THE TAN HILL INN

I was walking one morning along a Pennine summit when I saw an old man mending a drystone wall. It was a glorious day; the hills shone green near at hand, blue in the distance. I nodded to the old chap and said: "Fine morning." He gave me a glance of scorn and said witheringly: "Well, don't let's get into a lather about it."

PHYLLIS BENTLEY

There was a university in York when Oxford was just a place where cattle walked across a muddy river.

ROY HATTERSLEY

A Bradfordian was describing a visit to London to someone who had not been there before. "Well owd ad, tha's bin to Leeds, an't tha? Weel, it's like that – only wuss."

W R Mitchell

Hen 'oils, clogs an' home-fed bacon;
dry bread, wicket wi' corky balls;
summer suns an' speckled
birds' eggs;
chips – wi' bits on; cuckoo calls
Parkin, bullseyes, thick
spanish juice;
savvery ducks wi' a sting o' spice;
rowly poly puddins tumblin;
aht o' t' cloth all jammy and nice.

TRADITIONAL

The peace which I always found in the silence and emptiness of the moors filled me utterly.

JAMES HERRIOT (ALF WIGHT)

Folk are like tea. You can nivver judge o' their quality till they get into hot watter.

OLD AMOS

Did you know?

Leeds-born Barbara Taylor Bradford has sold ninety-two million copies of her books worldwide in more than ninety countries and they have been translated into forty languages.

I love Yorkshire, particularly the ruggedness of its landscape and bluntness of its people. Whenever I went on the moors and dales, I would feel the drama of the winds, and imagine the tortured gypsy figure of Heathcliff sweeping away on horseback. And I love the famous sons and daughters of Yorkshire, mainly because they are highly irritating but absolutely marvellous.

SIR DAVID TANG, HONG KONG

BUSINESSMAN

The problem is that I'm addicted to Yorkshire Tea, and for me, nothing else can really hit the spot. I like it very strong – my grandmother used to say that with a good cup of tea you could stand the spoon up in it. I used to use two teabags in a cup, although I've weaned myself down to one now... But there's no taking the teabag out of the cup or anything – it stays there till the tea is somewhere between dark brown and orange. I take Yorkshire Tea with me wherever I go.

BILL NIGHY

This part of northern England surely deserves to be considered not only Europe's leading destination, but possibly the greatest place on Earth.

CNN.COM

"God, it's all so irresistible."
PRINCE CHARLES IN A YORKSHIRE
DALES CHEESE SHOP

Fatther, fill mi mahth wi'
worthwhile stuff,

An nudge me when Ah've
etten enough.

TRADITIONAL

I'm scared of making generalisations, but there's a brusque, down-to-earth humour where people tend to hit the nail on the head. That accent lends itself to a dry wit and I like to say things funnily, rather than not funnily. I suppose if you say things in a very broad Yorkshire accent, people laugh anyway. Even if it's not funny.

SALLY WAINWRIGHT

Tell someone that you live, or have lived, in Leeds, and they are quite likely to say, "Well, it's easy to get out of."

ALAN BENNETT

Well, o' course, we had it tough.
We used to 'ave to get up out of
shoebox at twelve o'clock at night
and lick road clean wit' tongue. We
had two bits of cold gravel, worked
twenty-four hours a day at mill for
sixpence every four years, and when
we got home our dad would slice us
in two wit' bread knife.

YORKSHIREMAN, *AT LAST THE
1948 SHOW*

Right. I had to get up in the morning at ten o'clock at night, half an hour before I went to bed, drink a cup of sulphuric acid, work twenty-nine hours a day down mill and pay mill owner for permission to come to work, and when we got home, our dad and our mother would kill us and dance about on our graves singing Hallelujah.

YORKSHIREMAN, *AT LAST THE 1948 SHOW*

Definition of twerk

1. To dance in a provocative manner, using thrusting hip movements and a low, squatting stance.

2. Where people in Yorkshire go Monday to Friday, 9am–5pm.

A Symphony for Yorkshire

Sing a song of Yorkshire, from the
Humber to the Tees

Of horses, wool and terriers, of
pudding and of cheese.

I know no other county where the
land is quite so fine;

England's lovely county. And I'm
proud to call it mine.

Where shining purple heather

stretches far across the moor,
And the lapwing's cry above me
takes the place of traffic roar
And peace comes drifting gently,
there's no place I'd rather be
Than this land of hills and valleys,
from the Pennines to the sea.

So when I've done my roaming, and
when my step grows slow;
When heart and mind assure me

that the time has come to go,

Then let me rest in Yorkshire, for it's
there I want to lie

'neath sun and wind and heather...
and a gleaming Yorkshire sky.

**DOREEN BRIGHAM, WINNER OF
BBC COMPETITION TO FIND A
SYMPHONY FOR YORKSHIRE**

I'm so happy to be able to make it to Hull and we've already set up a date to the Yorkshire pudding factory! I love a fresh-baked Yorkshire pudding.

KATY PERRY

As a boy I was once nearly run down by an articulated lorry that carried the slogan "Have a break, have a KitKat", and it occurred to me that, as a northern death, it could not compare with being lost in a trawler off Hull or buried under a collapsed coalface.

ANDREW MARTIN

Who can possibly respect a part of the country [the south] where they can only eat fish and chips with the aid of a little wooden fork? If God had meant us to eat la-di-da, he would not have given us fingers.

ROY HATTERSLEY

Soon it'll be like Woodstock: people will pretend they were there – people will want to say, "I was there when it all started."

IAN MCMILLAN ON THE INAUGURAL YORKSHIRE PUDDING BOAT RACE IN 1999